DF_DC

Diese Buchreihe versammelt die Bauwerke einzelner, mit hohem Qualitätsanspruch ausgewählter jüngerer Schweizer Architektinnen und Architekten. Seit 2004 kuratiere ich die Reihe *Anthologie* in der Form einfacher Werkdokumentationen. Sie ist vergleichbar mit der «Blütenlese», wie sie in der Literatur für eine Sammlung ausgewählter Texte angewendet wird. Es liegt in der Natur des Architektenberufs, dass die Erstlingswerke meist kleinere übersichtliche Bauaufgaben sind. Sie sind eine Art Fingerübung, mit der sie das Erlernte anwenden und ihr architektonisches Sensorium erproben und entfalten können. Die Begabung und die Leidenschaft für das Metier lassen sich dabei früh in voller Deutlichkeit und Frische erkennen. So stecken in jedem der kleinen und grossen Projekte inspirierte Grundgedanken und Vorstellungen, die spielerisch und gleichermassen perfekt in architektonische Bilder, Formen und Räume umgesetzt werden. Damit wird mir wieder einmal bewusst, dass in der Architektur wie in anderen Kunstformen die Bilder und Ideen, die hinter dem Werk stehen, das Wesentliche sind. Es mag diese Intuition sein, die Kunstschaffende haben und die dann über ihr Werk wie ein Funke auf die Betrachtenden überspringt, so, wie es der italienische Philosoph Benedetto Croce in seinen Schriften eindringlich beschreibt.

Heinz Wirz
Verleger

This book series presents buildings by selected young Swiss architects that set themselves high quality standards. Since 2004, I have been curating the *Anthologie* series by simply documenting their oeuvre. The series can be compared to a literary anthology presenting a collection of selected texts. It is in the nature of the architectural profession that early works by young architects are mostly small, limited building tasks. They are a kind of five-finger exercise in which the architects apply what they have learnt, as well as testing and developing their architectural instincts. Talent and a passion for the profession can be seen at an early stage in all of its clarity and freshness. Each project, be it large or small, contains an inspired underlying concept and ideas that are playfully and consummately implemented as architectural images, forms and spaces. Thus, I am regularly reminded that in architecture, as in other art forms, the images and ideas behind the works are their essence. Perhaps this is the same intuition described so vividly by the Italian philosopher Benedetto Croce, one that is absorbed by the artist and flies like a spark via the work to the viewer.

Heinz Wirz
Publisher

DF_DC

QUART

POETIK DES MÖGLICHEN

Andrew Clancy

Architektur wird durch Kräfte ausserhalb ihrer selbst ins Leben gerufen. Ihre Gebäude werden unter Einhaltung der von der Bürokratie erlassenen Vorschriften mit Materialien errichtet, die mit dem kulturellen Desinteresse des Marktes dargeboten werden. Sie bilden den Rahmen für Ereignisse, Rituale und Prozesse, die die ganze Bandbreite menschlicher Erfahrung umfassen. Das Wissen unserer Disziplin ist angesiedelt in der Kulturgeschichte dieser im Laufe der Zeit gebauten Aushandlung, in den Sprachen und Formen, die uns die Geschichte darbietet. Diese Aushandlung zwischen Ideal und Wirklichkeit mindert die architektonische Autonomie nicht, sie ist vielmehr ein wesentlicher Abrieb – ebenso fruchtbar wie frustrierend. Hier vermag Architektur, Kritikfähigkeit zu entwickeln.

Vielleicht ist diese Aushandlung heute offensichtlicher als früher. Architekturschaffende werden in zunehmendem Masse dazu aufgefordert, gewöhnliche Gegenstände zu erarbeiten – Gebäude ebenso wie Denkmäler. Hier bekommt jegliche architektonische Intention Gewicht – ob durch den Einbezug vorgefundener Bedingungen, durch eine bestimmte Sprache oder rein abstrakte Absicht. Die Bandbreite der in diesem Band vorgestellten Arbeiten von DF_DC reicht von Umbauten bis hin zu frei stehenden Strukturen. Es gibt einen roten Faden – einen sich durch die verschiedenen Bereiche hindurchziehenden strategischer Ansatz, der die kontingenten Realitäten des Kontexts beugen und absorbieren kann. Die Sprache dieses Werkes ist der strategischen Intention untergeordnet und ergibt sich aus einer genauen Lektüre des Kontextes in Bezug auf Materialität und Form. Hinter dieser oberflächlichen Vielfalt wird jedoch immer wieder Sorge getragen für die Klarheit und Ordnung der äusseren Form; und es stellt sich die Frage, wie diese bei der Herstellung brillanter innerer Landschaften gegeneinander ausgespielt werden könnten. Die Poesie entsteht aus einer unerwarteten Gegenüberstellung der Dinge, im Spiel zwischen Lesbarkeit und Bewohnen, in den Momenten, in denen die Ordnung gebrochen oder gebeugt wird, um auf die Besonderheiten eines Ortes oder Programms zu reagieren.

Hier sehen wir keine strenge Autonomie, sondern eine kontinuierliche, kontingente Auseinandersetzung mit der Situation des jeweiligen Projekts – und das der Architekturgeschichte innewohnende Potenzial, eine Poetik des Möglichen zu finden.

POETICS OF THE POSSIBLE

Andrew Clancy

Architecture is called into being by forces outside itself. Its buildings are assembled to respect regulations set by bureaucrats using materials offered with the cultural disinterest of the market. They enclose events, rituals and processes which embrace the full breadth of human experience. The knowledge of our discipline is sited in the cultural history of this built negotiation over time, in the languages and forms presented to us from history. This negotiation between ideal and real is not a diminution of architectural autonomy – rather it is an essential abrasion which is as fruitful as it is frustrating. It is here that architecture finds its site to develop criticality.

Perhaps today this negotiation is more apparent than before. Architects are increasingly asked to work on ordinary things – the fabric as well as the monuments. Here the weight of any architectural intention gains its valency as much from harnessing found conditions as it is in driving a particular language or abstract intention. In this volume detailing the work of DF_DC, we are presented with work ranging from alterations to existing buildings to free standing structures. There is a thread throughout that we can trace, one which engages with its diverse territories first via a strategic approach that can inflect and absorb the contingent realities of the context. The language of the work is subsidiary to the strategic intention and is derived from a close reading of the context in terms of materiality and form. Throughout this superficial diversity however, there is a recurrent concern with the clarity and order of the external form, and of how this might be played against in the making of luminous interior landscapes. The poetry arises in the unexpected juxtaposition of things, in the play between legibility and habitation, in moments when the order is broken or inflected to respond to a particularity of the site or programme.

Here we see not austere autonomy, but rather a continual contingent engagement with the situation of each project, and the resonant potentials of the history of architecture to find a poetics of the possible.

APARTMENTGEBÄUDE, VIA CARONA, PARADISO
Ausführung 2017–2020

Das Gebäude reagiert in seiner Formgebung auf den schwierigen Standort an einer Bahnstrecke und kann auf verschiedenen Ebenen erschlossen werden. Es umfasst 14 Wohnungen auf fünf Ebenen, die über die langen Nordterrassen sukzessive den Blick auf den Luganer See freigeben. Das Projekt ist eine Ansammlung von Elementen mit unterschiedlicher Lebensdauer: Struktur, Haustechnik und Trennwände nehmen die Szenarien vorweg, wie sich das Gebäude im Laufe der Zeit verändern könnte. Durch die Anordnung ergibt sich eine Reihe eigentümlicher Typologien. Die Struktur neigt sich nach aussen, um im oberen Bereich ein auskragendes Element zu tragen, in dem sich das Penthouse befindet. Das verändert die Wahrnehmung des Gebäudes und der Landschaft im Hintergrund. Platten aus gehämmertem Beton füllen den Gebäuderahmen und weichen so den monolithischen Charakter des Gebäudes in materieller Hinsicht auf.

APARTMENT BUILDING, VIA CARONA, PARADISO
Construction 2017–2020

The building takes its form from the difficult site along the railway and articulates accesses at different levels. It contains 14 apartments over five levels, gradually revealing close views of Lake Lugano through the long northern terraces. The project is conceived as an assemblage of elements with different lifespans: structure, services and partitions, pre-empting the scenarios in which it might transform over time. The massing produces a range of peculiar typologies. The structure tilts out to support a projecting element at the top with the penthouse, changing the perception of the frame and the landscape beyond. Materially, bush-hammered concrete panels fill in the building's frame, thereby softening its monolithic character.

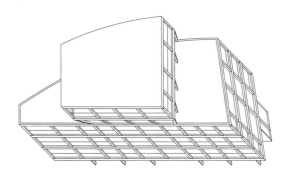

10 m

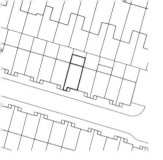

MEWS HOUSE, LONDON
Ausführung 2018–2020

Für eine Familie wurde im Westen Londons an einem Stallgebäude aus den 1980er Jahren eine Reihe kleinerer Eingriffe vorgenommen: eine Erweiterung im hinteren Bereich und auf dem Dach, eine Veränderung der Geschosshöhen und die Neugestaltung von Teilen des Grundrisses. Als verbindendes Element der strukturellen und räumlichen Interventionen dienen Rahmenelemente aus Hartholz, die verschiedene Formen annehmen: Decken, Trennwände, Vorbauten. Der zentrale Wohnbereich, dem eine der bisherigen Typologie fehlende Grösse und schmucklose Würde innewohnt, öffnet sich auf der Rückseite zu einem kleinen Innenhof.

MEWS HOUSE, LONDON
Construction 2018–2020

The project is a series of interventions on a 1980s mews house for a family in west London. These minor amendments include extending to the rear and on the roof, changing floor levels and reconfiguring parts of the plan. Frame elements in hardwood are introduced as a common language for the structural and spatial intervention, taking several guises in the process – roofs, screens, porches. The main living area gains a scale and unadorned dignity previously missing in the typology, opening up to a small patio in the back.

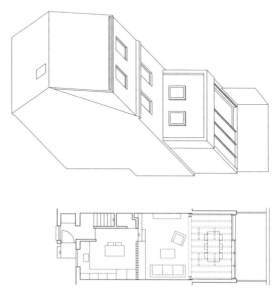

5 m

PYRAMID HOUSE, TEGNA
Ausführung 2018–2020

In diesem vorstädtischen Kontext erscheint das Haus als Fremdkörper von schwer fassbarer Grösse und faszinierendem Charakter. Im Inneren überrascht die Anordnung des L-förmigen Grundrisses unter den Schrägdächern und um den Garten herum. Sie steht im Gegensatz zur hermetischen Haltung des Baukörpers im Stadtgefüge. Die Serie grundrissbasierter Raumformen auf beiden Etagen und die ausgeschnittenen Öffnungen im Bereich der Schlafzimmer lassen sich von aussen kaum erahnen und treten lediglich vom Garten aus in Erscheinung. Von den angrenzenden Weinbergen aus betrachtet, erhebt sich das Haus als monumentale, introvertierte Form.

PYRAMID HOUSE, TEGNA
Construction 2018–2020

In its suburban context, the house appears as an extraneous object of a scale difficult to gauge and of intriguing character. Once inside, one is surprised by how the L-shaped plan is arranged underneath the pitched roofs and around the garden in opposition to the hermetic urban stance. The series of spatial forms on the two floors resulting from the section, together with the carved openings in the bedrooms, do not reveal much to the outside and only become evident from the garden. From the adjacent vineyards, the house rises as a monumental, introverted form.

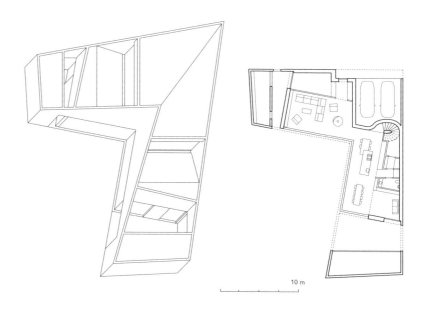

10 m

QUART

HIGHLIGHTS

2020/2

Peter Märkli – Everything one invents is true

Peter Märkli zählt seit den frühen 1980er-Jahren zweifellos zu den markantesten Deutschschweizer Architekten der ersten Stunde. Seine einprägsamen Bauten lassen sich jedoch nicht leicht in das Schema dieser Architekturbewegung einordnen. Zu sehr sind die einzelnen Bauwerke intensiv bearbeitete Individuen, die einer fortdauernden Bewegung des Suchens folgen. Immer eröffnen sie eigenständig und eindringlich Verbindungen der Geschichte der Architektur mit dem Impetus einer zeitüber-dauernden Gültigkeit.

Im vorliegenden Band sind 17 Bauten der letzten 15 Jahre mit Texten, Plänen und Abbildungen ausführlich dargestellt. Ergänzt wird die bemerkenswerte Werkdarstellung mit erhellenden Essays von Florian Beigel & Philip Christou, Franz Wanner und Ellis Woodman. Ein spannendes Interview mit Peter Märkli von Elena Markus und einzelne Statements des Architekten runden die eindrückliche Sammlung ab.

Herausgegeben von Pamela Johnston
Textbeiträge: Florian Beigel & Philip Christou, Pamela Johnston, Peter Märkli, Elena Markus, Franz Wanner, Ellis Woodman

240 Seiten, 29 × 29 cm
178 Abbildungen, 75 Pläne,
101 Zeichnungen
Hardcover, fadengeheftet
Englisch (teilweise übersetzt ins Deutsche *):
ISBN 978-3-03761-138-8
Englisch (teilweise übersetzt ins Japanische **):
ISBN 978-3-03761-139-5
CHF 138.– / EUR 126.–
* eingelegtes Booklet mit Essays in Deutsch
** eingelegtes Booklet mit Projektbeschrieben in Japanisch

Peter Märkli – Everything one invents is true

Since the early 1980s, Peter Märkli has been one of the most striking protagonists of German Swiss architecture from the earliest period of its emergence. However his impressive buildings cannot be easily classified in the scheme of this architectural movement, since the individual buildings are intensely developed individuals that follow the continuous movement of seeking. They always open up connections with the history of architecture in an independent, powerful way and express the impetus of timeless validity.

This volume presents 17 buildings in detail from the last 15 years with texts, plans and images. The remarkable presentation of works is complemented by enlightening essays by Florian Beigel & Philip Christou, Franz Wanner and Ellis Woodman. An exciting interview with Peter Märkli by Elena Markus and individual statements by the architects round off the impressive collection.

Edited by: Pamela Johnston
Articles by: Florian Beigel & Philip Christou, Pamela Johnston, Peter Märkli, Elena Markus, Franz Wanner, Ellis Woodman

240 pages, 29 × 29 cm
178 illustrations, 75 plans,
101 sketches
Hardback, thread-stitched
English (some texts also in German *):
ISBN 978-3-03761-138-8
English (some texts also in Japanese **):
ISBN 978-3-03761-139-5
CHF 138.00 / EUR 126.00
* with an enclosed booklet containing the essays in German
** with an enclosed booklet containing the project texts in Japanese

Gion A. Caminada

Von Gion A. Caminada ist in der bündnerischen Surselva ein architektonisches Werk entstanden, das wie kein anderes unmittelbar in den ökonomischen, geografischen und bautechnischen Prämissen eines Ortes und den Lebensgewohnheiten seiner Bevölkerung bedingt ist.

Die neue Buchausgabe umfasst die Texte und die Projektsammlung des Bandes Cul zuffel e l'aura dado und ist erweitert um eine Auswahl der neueren Projekte seit 2005.

Herausgegeben von: Bettina Schlorhaufer
Fotos: Lucia Degonda
Textbeiträge: Gion A. Caminada, Jürg Conzett, Bettina Schlorhaufer, Peter Schmid, Martin Tschanz, Peter Rieder, Walter Zschokke

2., mit neuen Projekten erweiterte Auflage des Bandes Cul zuffel e l'aura dado

296 Seiten, 22,5 × 29 cm
296 Abbildungen, 214 Skizzen/Pläne
Hardcover, fadengeheftet
Deutsch/Englisch
ISBN 978-3-03761-114-2
CHF 138.– / EUR 126.–

Gion A. Caminada

Gion A. Caminada has produced architectural work in Surselva, Grisons that is unique in being directly determined by the ecological, geographical and structural engineering premises of the location and the lifestyles of its population.

The new edition includes the texts and project collection of Cul zuffel e l'aura dado and is extended to include a selection of more recent projects since 2015.

Herausgegeben von: Bettina Schlorhaufer.
Fotos: Lucia Degonda. Textbeiträge: Jürg Conzett,
Peter Schmid, Peter Rieder, Walter Zschokke

2nd edition of Cul zuffel e l'aura dado, extended to include new projects

296 pages, 22.5 × 29 cm
296 illustrations,
214 sketeches/plans
Hardback, thread-stitched
German/English
ISBN 978-3-03761-114-2
CHF 138.00 / EUR 126.00

20 Onsitestudio – Mailand/Milan

In Mailand formiert sich eine Szene jüngerer Architekten, zu denen auch Onsitestudio mit den Protagonisten Giancarlo Floridi und Angelo Lunati zählt. Ihre Bauten sind von einer starken integrativen Kraft und urbanen Ausstrahlung geprägt und werden so zu einem wertvollen, stimmigen Teil des Mailänder Grossstadtgefüges.
Textbeiträge: Vittorio Magnago Lampugnani, Federico Tranfa

80 Seiten, 22,5 × 29 cm, 107 Abbildungen, 47 Pläne
Fadengeheftete Broschur, CHF 48.– / EUR 44.–
Deutsch/Englisch ISBN 978-3-03761-215-6

A young architectural scene is developing in Milan, including onsitestudio with its protagonists Giancarlo Floridi and Angelo Lunati. Their buildings are characterised by a strong integrative force, making them a valuable, coherent part of Milan's metropolitan fabric.
Articles by: Vittorio Magnago Lampugnani, Federico Tranfa

80 pages, 22.5 × 29 cm, 107 illustrations, 47 plans
Thread-stitched brochure
CHF 48.00 / EUR 44.00
German/English ISBN 978-3-03761-215-6

21 AFF Architekten – Berlin/Lausanne

Dauerhaftigkeit und Langlebigkeit von Formen, Bildern und Narrativen sind die architektonischen Themen, die Martin Fröhlich und Sven Fröhlich seit 2000 leidenschaftlich verfolgen. Daraus sind überraschende, starke und einprägsame Architekturen entstanden, die in ihrer Erscheinung und ihrem Ausdruck oft nahe der Konzeptkunst und der Minimalart liegen.
Textbeitrag: Hartmut Frank

72 Seiten, 22,5 × 29 cm, 102 Abbildungen, 33 Pläne
Fadengeheftete Broschur, CHF 48.– / EUR 44.–
Deutsch/Englisch ISBN 978-3-03761-241-5

Martin and Sven Fröhlich have passionately pursued the permanence and longevity of forms, images and narratives in architecture since 2000. The result is surprising, strong and memorable architecture that often appears close to conceptual and minimal art.
Articles by: Hartmut Frank

72 pages, 22.5 × 29 cm, 102 images, 30 plans
Thread-stitched brochure
CHF 48.00 / EUR 44.00
German/English ISBN 978-3-03761-241-5

85 Sylla Widmann

Starke, einprägsame Architekturen sind die Antworten auf vielfältige Bedingungen und Vorgaben. Sie sind erdacht und entwickelt vom Genfer Architektenpaar Kristina Sylla Widmann und Marc Widmann. Im vorliegenden Band sind fünf Schulbauten und Schulanlagen von hoher architektonischer Qualität sowie mehrere herausragende Wohn- und Verwaltungsbauten dargestellt.
Textbeitrag: Andrea Bassi

80 Seiten, 22,5 × 29 cm, 72 Abbildungen, 48 Pläne
Fadengeheftete Broschur, CHF 48.– / EUR 44.–
Deutsch/Englisch ISBN 978-3-03761-217-0
Französisch/Englisch ISBN 978-3-03761-240-8

Powerful, memorable architecture in response to diverse conditions and briefs, conceived and developed by the Geneva architectural couple Kristina Sylla Widmann and Marc Widmann: this volume presents five school buildings and facilities with a high architectural quality, as well as several outstanding residential and administrative buildings.
Article by: Andrea Bassi

80 pages, 22.5 × 29 cm, 72 illustrations, 48 plans
Thread-stitched brochure
CHF 48.00 / EUR 44.00
German/English ISBN 978-3-03761-217-0
French/English ISBN 978-3-03761-240-8

43 Lilitt Bollinger Studio

2013 gründete Lilitt Bollinger in Nuglar in der Nähe Basels ihr eigenes Büro. Seither sind einige erlesene Umbauten entstanden, die ganz aus der Atmosphäre des Gebäudes und des Orts entwickelt sind. Durch die ausgesprochene Affinität zu Konstruktion und räumlichem Ausdruck erzeugen ihre Gebäude ihre einzigartige Stimmung.

52 Seiten, 16,5 × 21 cm, 40 Abbildungen, 12 Pläne
Fadengeheftete Broschur, CHF 28.– / EUR 25.–
Deutsch/Englisch ISBN 978-3-03761-222-4

In 2013, Lilitt Bollinger founded her own office in Nuglar near Basel. Since then, the office has produced a number of refined conversions that are entirely developed out of the atmosphere of the building and location. The pronounced affinity to construction and spatial expression gives the buildings their unique atmosphere.

52 pages, 16.5 × 21 cm, 40 images, 12 plans
Thread-stitched brochure
CHF 28.00 / EUR 25.00
German/English ISBN 978-3-03761-222-4

Zürcher Wohnungsbau 1995–2015

Seit Mitte der 1990er Jahre lässt sich im Grossraum Zürich eine ausserordentliche Qualität von Wohnbauten beobachten. Durch die Förderung der öffentlichen Hand, durch eine hochstehende Wettbewerbskultur und eine rege Architekturszene ist hier ein reichhaltiges Experimentierfeld guter Wohnbauarchitektur entstanden. Das umfangreiche Werk über den Zürcher Wohnungsbau ist eine Anthologie von über 100 Einzelbauten, Ensembles und Siedlungen, die innerhalb von 20 Jahren in der Stadt Zürich entstanden sind. Es ist eine eindrückliche Übersicht zur Wohnbaukultur, die mit ihrer aussergewöhnlichen Qualität eine Intensität und Blüte erlebt, die auch international Beachtung findet.

Herausgeber: Heinz Wirz, Christoph Wieser

476 Seiten, 24 × 29 cm
710 Abbildungen, 713 Pläne
Hardcover, fadengeheftet
Deutsch/Englisch
ISBN 978-3-03761-127-2
CHF 138.– / EUR 126.–

Zurich Housing Development 1995–2015

Housing of exceptional quality has been developed in the greater Zurich area since the mid-1990s. Public funding, the high standard of the competition culture and a vibrant architectural scene have resulted in a rich field of experimentation for good residential architecture. The approximately 500-page volume on Zurich housing construction is an anthology of over 100 individual buildings, ensembles and settlements developed over a period of 20 years. It is an impressive representation of an intense, blossoming housing development culture that has also attracted international attention.

476 pages, 24 × 29 cm
710 illustrations, 713 plans
Hardback, thread-stitched
German/English
ISBN 978-3-03761-127-2
CHF 138.00 / EUR 126.00

Edited by: Heinz Wirz, Christoph Wieser

EVA WILLENEGGER LUKAS IMHOF PROFESSUR MIROSLAV ŠIK

ANALOGE ALTNEUE ARCHITEKTUR

Analoge Altneue Architektur

Analoge Architektur und Altneue Architektur prägen die Lehre von Miroslav Šik an der ETH Zürich. In der ersten Analogen Phase 1983–1991 assistiert Šik am Lehrstuhl Fabio Reinhart und ist faktisch Wortführer einer architektonischen Bewegung, die weit über die Schweizergrenze hinaus bekannt wird, die bis heute Wirkung zeigt. In der zweiten Altneuen Phase 1999–2018 realisiert Miroslav Šik als Entwurfsprofessor an der ETH Zürich eine Reformarchitektur mit Ensemble, Milieu-Stimmung und Midcomfort.

Der umfangreiche Band enthält insgesamt 135 ausgewählte studentische Projekte aus beiden Phasen, deren etliche Verfasser heute zu den namhaften Schweizer Architekten zählen. Grossformatige perspektivische Zeichnungen, Collagen, Pläne mit Detailtreue und prägnant formulierte Projektbeschreibungen veranschaulichen bildhaft die Methode und deren Ergebnisse.

Auf der Shortlist des Richard Schlagman Art Book Award 2019

474 Seiten, 21 × 29 cm
694 Abbildungen, 522 Pläne/Skizzen
Hardcover, fadengeheftet
Deutsch ISBN 978-3-03761-153-1
Englisch ISBN 978-3-03761-154-8
CHF 128.– / EUR 116.–

Herausgeber: Miroslav Šik, Eva Willenegger
Textbeiträge: Miroslav Šik, Lukas Imhof, Alberto Dell'Antonio, Andreas Hagmann, Christoph Mathys

Analogue Oldnew Architecture

The terms "analogue architecture" and "oldnew architecture" are key aspects of the teaching of Miroslav Šik at the ETH Zurich. During his first period there (1983–1991), Šik worked as Senior Assistant at the Chair of Fabio Reinhart and was in effect the spokesman of an architectural movement that became renowned far beyond the borders of Switzerland and is still influential today. Miroslav Šik worked as a Full Professor at the ETH Zurich between 1999 and 2018 during his second period there.

This extensive volume contains the best 135 works respectively by students from both periods of Miroslav Šik's teaching, including plans, project descriptions and perspective diagrams. Some of the presented students went on to become renowned contemporary Swiss architects.

Shortlisted for the Richard Schlagman Art Book Award 2019

474 pages, 21 × 29 cm
694 images, 522 plans/sketches
Hardback, thread-stitched
German ISBN 978-3-03761-153-1
English ISBN 978-3-03761-154-8
CHF 128.00 / EUR 116.00

Editor: Miroslav Šik, Eva Willenegger
Articles by: Miroslav Šik, Lukas Imhof, Alberto Dell'Antonio, Andreas Hagmann, Christoph Mathys

83 Baumberger & Stegmeier

Peter Baumberger und Karin Stegmeier gehören zu den jüngeren Architekten innerhalb des qualitätsvollen Zürcher Wohnungsbaus der letzten Jahre. Neben den Wohnbauten von hohem Raffinement sind auch inspirierte Gebäude wie etwa die Erweiterung der Schulanlage Dorf in Dietlikon oder die Erweiterung des Primarschulzentrums in Laufen entstanden.
Textbeiträge: Tibor Joanelly, Christoph Baumberger

84 Seiten, 22,5 × 29 cm, 103 Abbildungen, 41 Pläne
Fadengeheftete Broschur, CHF 48.– / EUR 44.–
Deutsch/Englisch ISBN 978-3-03761-097-8

**Peter Baumberger and Karin Stegmeier are young architects who have produced high-quality Zurich housing in recent years. In addition to their highly refined residential architecture, they have designed inspired buildings such as the extension to the Dietlikon village school or the extension to the primary school centre in Laufen.
Articles by: Tibor Joanelly, Christoph Baumberger**

84 pages, 22.5 × 29 cm, 103 illustrations, 41 plans
Thread-stitched brochure
CHF 48.00 / EUR 44.00
German/English ISBN 978-3-03761-097-8

84 Aebi & Vincent Architekten

Seit 1996 arbeiten die beiden Architekten Bernhard Aebi und Pascal Vincent in ihrem Büro in Bern. Es sind Sanierungen historischer Bauten wie etwas das Bundeshaus in Bern, aber auch zahlreiche Wohnbauten und Verwaltungsgebäude, die zumeist aus Wettbewerbserfolgen entstanden sind und eine durchwegs hohe architektonische Qualität aufweisen.
Textbeitrag: Christoph Schläppi

168 Seiten, 22,5 × 29 cm, 132 Abbildungen, 69 Pläne
Fadengeheftete Broschur, CHF 48.– / EUR 44.–
Deutsch/Englisch ISBN 978-3-03761-199-9

**The two Bern architects Bernhard Aebi and Pascal Vincent have designed an impressive portfolio of works since 1996, including renovations of historical buildings such as the Bundeshaus in Bern, but also many residential and administrative buildings, mostly following competition successes and always achieving great architectural qualities.
Article by: Christoph Schläppi**

168 pages, 22.5 × 29 cm, 132 illustrations, 69 plans
Thread-stitched brochure
CHF 48.00 / EUR 44.00
German/English ISBN 978-3-03761-199-9

5 Wege zum Raum

Der fünfte Band der Reihe Laboratorium spannt den Raum auf zwischen Themen und Positionen am Institut. Die Texte befassen sich mit vielfältigen Aspekten und Fragen zur Thematik des gebauten und wahrgenommenen Raums. Energiefragen, der Umgang mit dem urban-ländlichen Raum oder das Arbeiten mit Modellen werden reflektiert. Neben inhaltlichen Themen stehen Methoden und Herangehensweisen im Fokus.

Herausgegeben von: Hochschule Luzern – Technik & Architektur, Johannes Käferstein, Damaris Baumann
Vorwort: Johannes Käferstein
Texte von: Alberto Alessi, Peter Althaus, Heike Biechteler, Luca Deon, Yves Dusseiller, Angelika Juppien, Wolfgang Rossbauer, Lando Rossmaier, Annika Seifert, Felix Wettstein

136 Seiten, 17 × 22 cm, 87 Abbildungen, 15 Pläne
Fadengeheftete Broschur, CHF 34.– / EUR 31.–
Deutsch ISBN 978-3-03761-233-0

The fifth volume of the Laboratorium series spans the themes and positions at the institute. The texts address diverse aspects of and questions on the theme of developed and perceived space. Questions of energy, handling urban and rural spaces, and working with models are reflected upon. In addition to content-based themes, the book also examines methods and approaches.
Edited by: Lucerne University of Applied Sciences and Arts – Engineering & Architecture, Johannes Käferstein, Damaris Baumann
Foreword: Johannes Käferstein
Articles by: Alberto Alessi, Peter Althaus, Heike Biechteler, Luca Deon, Yves Dusseiller, Angelika Juppien, Wolfgang Rossbauer, Lando Rossmaier, Annika Seifert, Felix Wettstein

136 pages, 17 × 22 cm, 87 illustrations, 20 plans
Thread-stitched brochure
CHF 34.00 / EUR 31.00
German ISBN 978-3-03761-233-0

6 Durchdringung als Bedingung

Dieser Band nimmt den Abschluss der langjährigen Lehr- und Forschungstätigkeit von Dieter Geissbühler zum Anlass, der Bedeutung der Konstruktion in der Architektur nachzugehen. Die verschiedenen Beiträge beleuchten in einem collageartigen Aufbau die vor allem in der Lehre vertretene Haltung.

Herausgegeben von: Hochschule Luzern – Technik & Architektur; Johannes Käferstein, Dieter Geissbühler
Autor: Dieter Geissbühler
Vorwort: Viktor Sigrist
Texte von: Oliver Dufner, Christoph Flury, Uli Herres, Charlotte Hustinx, Johannes Käferstein, Andrea Kuhn, Stefan Kunz, Mario Rinke, Uwe Teutsch, Daniel Tschuppert, Felix Wettstein, Christoph Wieser

96 Seiten, 17 × 22 cm, 97 Abbildungen, 21 Pläne
Fadengeheftete Broschur, CHF 34.– / EUR 31.–
Deutsch ISBN 978-3-03761-235-4

This volume marks the conclusion of the many years of teaching and research by Dieter Geissbühler, investigating the significance of construction in architecture. The various articles are compiled in a collage-like structure and shed light on stances that have above all been communicated in teaching.
Edited by: Institute of Architecture, Lucerne University of Applied Sciences and Arts – Engineering & Architecture, Johannes Käferstein, Dieter Geissbühler
Author: Dieter Geissbühler
Foreword: Viktor Sigrist
Articles by: Oliver Dufner, Christoph Flury, Uli Herres, Charlotte Hustinx, Johannes Käferstein, Andrea Kuhn, Stefan Kunz, Mario Rinke, Uwe Teutsch, Daniel Tschuppert, Felix Wettstein, Christoph Wieser

96 pages, 17 × 22 cm, 97 illustrations, 21 plans
Thread-stitched brochure
CHF 34.00 / EUR 31.00
German ISBN 978-3-03761-235-4

Zentral- und Hochschulbibliothek Luzern
Denkmalpflegerische Erneuerung
Thomas Lussi, Remo Halter Casagrande

Im Herbst 2019 wurde die Restaurierung der denkmalgeschützten Bibliothek durch die Luzerner Architekten Thomas Lussi und Remo Halter Casagrande abgeschlossen. Die Architekten lösen in souveräner Art die komplexen Aufgaben, die einer denkmalpflegerischen Erneuerung heute zueigen sind: der optimale Erhalt der Substanz, das Aufdecken und Wiederherstellen der oft differenzierten, feinsinnigen Qualitäten des ursprünglichen Bauwerks, die vorsichtige statische Stabilisierung der Konstruktion und die behutsame, durch die Nutzung bedingte Erneuerungen einzelner Teilen im und am Gebäude. Das Originalbauwerk wurde nach einem Entwurf von Otto Dreyer – einer der wichtigsten Luzerner Architekten jener Zeit – 1951 erstellt.

Das Buch dokumentiert das Originalgebäude von 1951, gibt einen Einblick in die bauhistorische Analyse vor dem Umbau und beschreibt mit umfangreichem Plan- und Fotomaterial die Strategie und die Massnahmen der Architekten zur Erneuerung des architekturhistorisch bedeutenden Gebäudes.

Textbeiträge:
Cony Grünenfelder, Siegfried Moeri, Rudolf Mumenthaler, Ulrich Niederer, Stanislaus von Moos, u. a.
Fotos: Leonardo Finotti

136 Seiten, 22,5 × 29 cm
133 Abbildungen, 22 Pläne
Leinenband, fadengeheftet
Deutsch/Englisch
ISBN 978-3-03761-216-3
CHF 54.– / EUR 49.–

Lucerne Central and University Library
Heritage renovation
Thomas Lussi, Remo Halter Casagrande

In the autumn of 2019, the Lucerne architects Thomas Lussi and Remo Halter Casagrande completed the restoration of the preservation-listed library. The architects competently solve the complex tasks involved in heritage renovation today: the ideal preservation of the substance, discovering and restoring often nuanced, detailed qualities in the original building, the careful static stabilisation of the structure and the gentle renewal of individual elements as a result of use in and around the building. The original building was erected in 1951 according to plans by Otto Dreyer – one of the most important Lucerne architects of the time.

The book documents the original 1951 building, provides insight into the building-historical analysis before the renovation and uses extensive plans and photo material to describe the strategy and measures by the architects in restoring the architecturally important historical building.

Articles by:
Cony Grünenfelder, Siegfried Moeri, Rudolf Mumenthaler, Ulrich Niederer, Stanislaus von Moos et al.
Photos: Leonardo Finotti

136 pages, 22.5 × 29 cm
133 illustrations, 22 plans
Clothbound, thread-stitched
German/English
ISBN 978-3-03761-216-3
CHF 54.00 / EUR 49.00

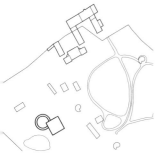

KUNSTPAVILLON, NANS-SOUS-SAINTE-ANNE, FRANKREICH
Ausführung 2021–2022

Die Vorgabe bestand darin, einen Pavillon für lokale Kunstschaffende und öffentliche Anlässe auf dem Gelände eines Schlosses in Ostfrankreich zu errichten. Um der Offenheit des Auftrags gerecht zu werden, sieht der Vorschlag zwei sich überschneidende Grundformen vor – einen Kreis und ein Quadrat. Sie sind als Raumpaar konzipiert, wobei sich der eine Raum zum Himmel und der andere zum Horizont hin öffnet. Beide können unabhängig voneinander oder gemeinsam genutzt werden. Dank seiner abstrakten Grundfläche präsentiert sich der Pavillon als ein weiteres Landschaftselement zwischen Bäumen, Wegen und landwirtschaftlichen Strukturen. Die Holzkonstruktion besteht aus Vierfachpfosten und durchgehenden Balken, die zu Standardelemente gefügt sind – und damit von den Einheimischen einfach errichtet werden können.

ARTS PAVILION, NANS-SOUS-SAINTE-ANNE, FRANCE
Construction 2021–2022

The brief asked for a pavilion for local artists and public gatherings in the grounds of a chateau in eastern France. To address the openness of the brief, the proposal is made of two intersected elemental forms – a circle and a square. Conceived as a couple of rooms, one open to the sky and one to the horizon, they can be used independently or in combination. Through this abstract footprint, the pavilion presents itself as one more landscape element along trees, paths and agricultural structures. The timber frame is formed of quadruple posts and continuous beams to standard modules, for straightforward erection by local people.

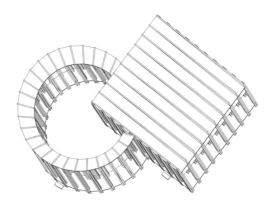

10 m

LEANING YUCCA HOUSE, LONDON
Ausführung 2017–2018

Bei diesem Projekt handelt es sich um die Neugestaltung und Erweiterung eines viktorianischen Reihenhauses im Nordwesten Londons. Um mit nur geringfügigen Erweiterungen mehr Platz zu schaffen, wurden die Hauptbereiche in einem Raum zusammengefasst und Elemente wie Küche, Treppe und Haustechnik in einem einzigen Block aus Eichenholz zusammengeführt. Ein zweites Schlüsselelement ist das grosse quadratische Fenster, das den Garten auf überraschende Weise in die Küche bringt, den Jahreszeitenwechsel in Szene setzt und die schiefe Yucca sowie den japanischen Ahorn im Hintergrund rahmt.

LEANING YUCCA HOUSE, LONDON
Construction 2017–2018

The project is a reconfiguration and extension of a semi-detached Victorian house in northwest London. In order to create more space with only a modest extension, the main areas are joined in one space, with elements such as the kitchen, staircase and utilities consolidated into a single oak joinery piece. A second key move was a large square window bringing the garden into the kitchen at an unexpectedly high level, magnifying the seasonal change and framing a leaning yucca and a Japanese maple in the background.

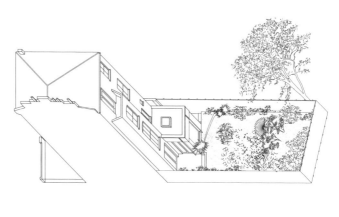

5 m

PALAZZO DEL CINEMA, LOCARNO

Ausführung 2015–2017 (mit AZPML, London; Wettbewerb 2012, 1. Preis)

Durch die Umwandlung einer ehemaligen Schule entstand ein audiovisuelles Zentrum. Es beherbergt drei Kinosäle, den Hauptsitz der Filmfestspiele, eine Filmhochschule, einen Mehrzwecksaal und andere Dienstleistungen rund um den Bereich Film.

Aus ökologischen Gründen sowie im Hinblick auf das historische Gedächtnis wurde das bestehende Gebäude erhalten. Der Logik der historischen Schichtung folgend, wurde lediglich eine Reihe punktueller Interventionen vorgenommen. Während die historischen Fassaden wiederhergestellt wurden, ist der Erweiterungsbau mit seiner goldenen kinetischen Fassade eindeutig zeitgenössisch geprägt. Die spartanische Innenausstattung der Büros steht im Kontrast zur neuen goldenen Eingangshalle, die als Erweiterung des öffentlichen Raumes gedacht ist.

PALAZZO DEL CINEMA, LOCARNO

Construction 2015–2017 (with AZPML, London; competition in 2012, 1st Prize)

The project is born from the transformation of the old public school into an audiovisual hub, comprising three cinema theatres, the Film Festival HQ, a film school, a multi-purpose hall and other services. For environment reasons and in view of historical memory, the project foresaw preserving the existing building through a series of local interventions, following the logic of historical stratification. The historical façades were refurbished, while the extension with its golden kinetic envelope is a clearly contemporary intervention. The spartan interiors of the offices contrasts with the new golden entrance hall, which has the effect of expanding the public space.

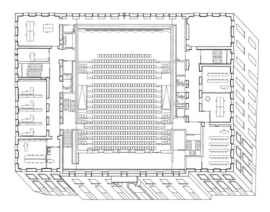

10 m

CHAPINAYA RETREAT, CHAPALASEE, MEXIKO
Ausführung 2021–2022

Der Auftrag sah vor, auf einem steil abfallenden Gelände mit Blick auf Mexikos grössten See einen asketischen Rückzugsort zu schaffen, der in enger Verbindung mit der Landschaft steht. Die topografische Strategie sieht eine Reihe verstreuter trapezförmiger Mauerpfeiler vor, von denen leichte Holzkabinen abgehängt sind. Diese sind dreigeteilt in Sitz-, Wasch- und Schlafbereich und weisen jeweils eine individuelle Gestaltung mit Bezug zur Topografie und Aussicht auf. In jeder Kabine werden die drei Räume durch eine halbautomatische Plattform verbunden, die den Mittelpunkt des jeweiligen Ensembles bildet und von der Privatsphäre und dem günstigen Klima profitiert.

CHAPINAYA RETREAT, LAKE CHAPALA, MEXICO
Construction 2021–2022

The site is a steep hillside overlooking the largest lake in Mexico and the brief is an austere refuge with a strong connection to the landscape. The topographic strategy is a series of scattered trabeated, angular masonry piers from which light timber cabins are suspended. The arrangement is tripartite: seating, bathing and sleeping areas, each one with a particular articulation responding to the topography and views. The three rooms in each cabin are connected by a semi-external platform as the focal point of the ensemble, benefitting from privacy and the clement weather.

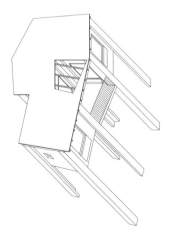

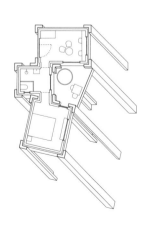

5 m

CONCRETE VILLA, COMANO
Ausführung 2017–2018

Die ungewöhnliche Typologie dieser Villa beruht auf zweierlei Faktoren: der malerischen Aussicht nach Osten und Westen und dem Wunsch, sich von den unmittelbar angrenzenden Nachbarbauten im Norden und Süden abzuschirmen. Sie evoziert damit das Bild einer bewohnten Mauer. Die Wohnbereiche auf der Rückseite weisen doppelte Raumhöhen auf und gehen in die Terrasse und den Pool über. Diese werden durch einen auskragenden Rahmen gefasst, der als raumbildendes Element fungiert. Tektonisch werden die langen Flanken durch eine Reihe von Pfeilern aus Ortbeton gegliedert, die sich abwechseln mit Platten in Strollato-Technik – eine alte Technik, die traditionell in lombardischen Villen zum Einsatz kam und bei der eine Mischung aus Kieseln und Zement mit einer Kelle von Hand aufgetragen und später geschliffen wird.

CONCRETE VILLA, COMANO
Construction 2017–2018

The peculiar typology results from having picturesque views to the east and west and a need to be shielded from nearby neighbours to the north and south, thus resembling an inhabited wall. The double-height living areas to the rear merge with the terrace and the pool and are tied back to the main volume by a projecting frame acting as a territorial device. Tectonically, the long flanks are articulated by a relief of in-situ concrete piers, separated by panels in *strollato* – an old technique of hand-applied mortar and aggregate traditionally used in Lombard villas.

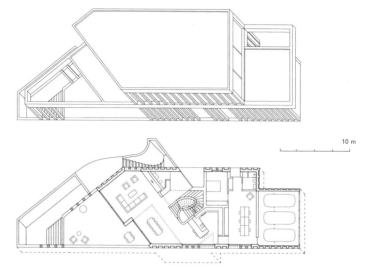

10 m

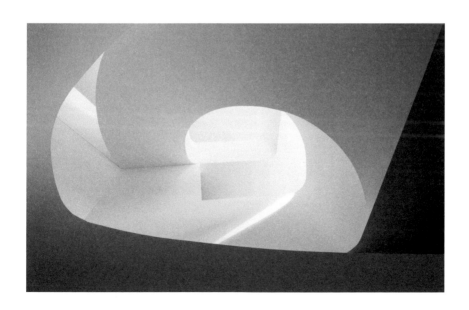

HOTEL STELLA, LUGANO
Ausführung 2021–2022

Bei diesem Projekt handelt es sich um die jüngste Umwandlung eines Hotels aus den frühen Jahren des 20. Jahrhunderts im Zentrum von Lugano, das sukzessive einer Reihe von kleinen Veränderungen unterzogen wurde. Die bestehende Figur hat eine «Neuerfindung» erfahren, indem die Zugangs- und Wegesituation sowie die Raumtypologien auf allen Stockwerken neu organisiert wurden. Zudem wurde das Schrägdach durch ein weiteres Stockwerk ersetzt. Die Fensteranordnung wurde rationalisiert und die Verbindung zur Strasse optimiert. Abgesehen von dieser Vereinfachung ist das Volumen nun von aussen gedämmt und grob verputzt, wodurch sich der historisch anmutende Baukörper durch eine abstraktere Präsenz besser in das Stadtbild einfügt. Auf der Rückseite des Gebäudes findet sich ein aus Fragmenten zusammengesetzter, stufenförmiger geheimer Garten.

HOTEL STELLA, LUGANO
Construction 2021–2022

The project is the latest transformation of an early 20th-century hotel in central Lugano, in a sequence of minor but constant alterations over time. A reinvention within the existing figure is achieved by redistributing access, circulation and room typologies across the floors, while replacing the pitched roof with a new storey. The fenestration grid is rationalised and access from the street is improved by relocating the entrance/lobby. Beyond this simplification, the volume is externally insulated and finished in *strollato*, balancing the historical character of the mass with a more abstract presence in the townscape. A secret, cascading garden is consolidated from fragments at the rear.

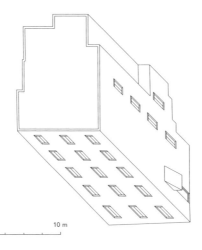

10 m

DOPPELHAUS, LOSONE
Ausführung 2020–2021

Die Form des Gebäudes ergibt sich aus seinem Grundstück an der Grenze zwischen historischem Kern und Erweiterung der Stadt. Dieser Übergang spiegelt sich in dem seltsamen L-förmigen Grundriss wider, der sich aus diversen Versätzen und anderen normativen Parametern ergibt. Der Gebäudekörper schwebt etwas über dem Boden – über Garage und Keller – und ermöglicht über die Einbauelemente, die am schmalsten Ende in Terassen übergehen, diverse Raumorganisationen. Das ungewohnte Volumen basiert auf einem regelmässigen Betonraster und gehämmerten Bossen, welche das Verhältnis von Flächen und Öffnungen typologisch organisieren.

DOUBLE HOUSE, LOSONE
Construction 2020–2021

The building takes its form from the location on the boundary between historical core and the town extension. This transition is reflected in the strange L-shaped plot, which the building adopts after applying the offsets and other normative parameters. Slightly hovering above the ground to accommodate the garage and cellars, the perimetral structure enables a variety of spatial arrangements for the dwellings using joinery elements, with terraces at the narrowest end. The unfamiliar volume is composed of a regular concrete grid and bush-hammered spandrels to regulate the apertures in relation to the internal space.

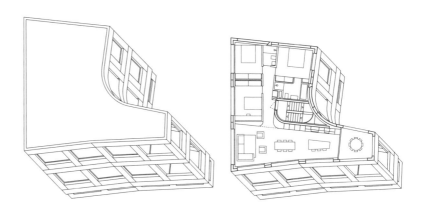

5 m

WERKVERZEICHNIS
Auswahl Bauten, Projekte und Wettbewerbe

1

2012	1	Black House, Cagiallo
2014		Mehrfamilienhaus, Agno
2015		Mehrfamilienhaus, Ascona
2016		Wohnung in Hampstead, London
2017		Palazzo del Cinema, Locarno (mit AZPML, London; Wettbewerb 2012, 1. Preis)
		Fussgängerbrücke Ex-Torretta, Bellinzona (mit AZPML, London; Wettbewerb 2016, 1. Preis)
	2	Brick House, Guadalajara, Mexiko
		Chapinaya Retreat, Chapalasee, Mexiko
2018		Concrete Villa, Comano
	3	Haus 1 am Elliott Square, London
		Leaning Yucca House, London
	4	Fünf Lofts, Muralto
	5	Wettbewerb Sporthalle, Terre di Pedemonte
		Künstleratelier, Camorino
	6	Wohnhaus, Muzzano
2019		Camden Mews House, London
		Wohnhaus, Tesserete
	7	Inselmasterplan & Retreat, Mozambique
		Tavazzano-Quartier, Mailand
	8	Wettbewerb Erweiterung Kantonsgericht, Lausanne (mit Morris+Company); 7. Preis
		Masterplan für den Parco Gerretta, Bellinzona
	9	Haus im Garten, Brighton
		Schulgebäude, Lamone
2020		Schulgebäude, West Hampstead, London
		Kunstpavillion, Nans-sous-Sainte-Anne, Frankreich
		Haus II am Elliott Square, London
	10	Wettbewerb Schule und Sporthalle, Magliaso
		Mews House, London
		Haus El Palomar, Guadalajara, Mexiko
		Pyramid House, Tegna
		Mehrfamilienhaus, Via Carona, Paradiso

2

3

Laufende Projekte
Doppelhaus, Losone
Hotel Stella, Lugano

4

5

6

7

8

LIST OF WORKS
Selection of buildings, projects and competitions

Current projects
Double House, Losone
Hotel Stella, Lugano

9

10

DARIO FRANCHINI

1983	geboren in Ascona
2002–2007	Praktikum bei Ennio Magetti, Minusio
2007	Diplom, Accademia di Architettura, Mendrisio (Preis der Stadt Olten)
2007–2009	Mitarbeit bei AuS Architecture & Urban Systems, Mendrisio
2008	Mitglied OTIA (Ordine ingegneri e architetti del Cantone Ticino)
2009	Gründung von DF Dario Franchini in Lugano
2011–2012	Assistent bei Frédéric Bonnet, Accademia di Architettura, Mendrisio
2015	Mitglied SIA
seit 2016	Büro mit Diego Calderon
2016	Mitglied REG A
seit 2018	Leitung eines Studios an der Kingston University, London

DIEGO CALDERON

1984	geboren in San Luis Potosi, Mexiko
2002	Architekturstudium, ITESM, Mexiko
2004	Architekturstudium, Accademia di Architettura, Mendrisio
2002–2005	Praktika bei JC Name, Guadalajara, und Aires Mateus, Lissabon
2008	Diplom, Accademia di Architettura, Mendrisio (Preis der Stadt Padua)
2008–2010	Mitarbeit bei Jonathan Woolf Architects, London
2010–2016	Mitarbeit bei Duggan Morris Architects, London
2013	Promotion, Accademia di Architettura, Mendrisio
2016	Mitglied ARB & RIBA
seit 2016	Leitung eines Studios an der Kingston University, London
seit 2016	Büro mit Dario Franchini

MITARBEITENDE

Lugano	Paolo Crippa, Federica Zoboli, Silvia Passiglia, Nicola Andreani, Gianfranco Panza, Laura Vilalta Ibañez, Silke Schnidrig, Veronica Marzorati, Nicole Vairetti
London	Mathias Broniatowski, Diego Palomares Gaspar (Zusammenarbeit), Victor Perlheden, Sebastián Alvarez, Maria Teresa Albano, Felix Everard, Veronica Casey-Fierro, Priya Kana, Radina Todorova

DARIO FRANCHINI

1983	Born in Ascona, Switzerland
2002–2007	Internship at Ennio Magetti, Minusio
2007	Diploma at the Accademia di Architettura, Mendrisio (City of Olten Award)
2007–2009	Employed at AuS Architecture & Urban Systems, Mendrisio
2008	OTIA member
2009	Founded DF Dario Franchini in Lugano
2011–2012	Assistant at the atelier Frédéric Bonnet, Accademia di Archittettura, Mendrisio
2015	SIA member
2016	REG A member
since 2016	Joint office with Diego Calderon
since 2018	Studio leader at Kingston University, London

DIEGO CALDERON

1984	Born in San Luis Potosi, Mexico
2002	Studied Architecture at ITESM, Mexico
2004	Studied Architecture at the Accademia di Architettura, Mendrisio
2002–2005	Internships at JC Name, Guadalajara and Aires Mateus, Lisbon
2008	Diploma at the Accademia di Architettura, Mendrisio (City of Padova Award)
2008–2010	Employed at Jonathan Woolf Architects, London
2010–2016	Employed at Duggan Morris Architects, London
2013	PhD studies at the Accademia di Architettura, Mendrisio
2016	Member of ARB & RIBA
since 2016	Studio leader at Kingston University, London
since 2016	Joint office with Dario Franchini

EMPLOYEES

Lugano	Paolo Crippa, Federica Zoboli, Silvia Passiglia, Nicola Andreani, Gianfranco Panza, Laura Vilalta Ibañez, Silke Schnidrig, Veronica Marzorati, Nicole Vairetti
London	Mathias Broniatowski, Diego Palomares Gaspar (collaborator), Victor Perlheden, Sebastián Alvarez, Maria Teresa Albano, Felix Everard, Veronica Casey-Fierro, Priya Kana, Radina Todorova

AUSZEICHNUNGEN

2008	*Preis der Stadt Olten* (Diplomprojekt, Mendrisio)
2009	*Preis der Stadt Padua* (Diplomprojekt, Mendrisio)
2019	Lobende Erwähnung (Concrete Villa, Comano), National Academy of Architecture, Mexiko

AUSSTELLUNGEN

2013	*Barcelona_Import Ticino*, COAC, Barcelona
2017	*Schweizweit. Recent Architecture in Switzerland*, Schweizerisches Architekturmuseum, Basel
	Schweizweit. Recent Architecture in Switzerland, Arc en Rêve, Bordeaux
	Schweizweit. Recent Architecture in Switzerland, Ex-Macello, Lugano
2019	Architekturbiennale im Bundesstaat Jalisco, Guadalajara, Mexiko
	Transcriptions. From Literary to Architectural Space, Juan-Jose-Arreola-Bibliothek, Guadalajara, Mexiko

BIBLIOGRAFIE

2012	[Wettbewerbsbeitrag zur Ticino Electrical Company]. In: Archi, Nr. 6, S. 75
2013	[Palazzo del Cinema]. In: Hochparterre, Nr. 1, S. 66
	SAMSTA, Architects Journal, in: *Architects Journal*, Mai
	[Palazzo del Cinema]. In: Neue Zürcher Zeitung, 17. August
	[Black House Cagiallo]. In: Barcelona Import Ticino. Architecture & Territory, COAC, S. 72–75
2017	[Mehrfamilienhaus in Ascona]. In: Schweizweit. Recent Architecture in Switzerland. Basel, S. 86–87
	[Palazzo del Cinema]. In: Neue Zürcher Zeitung, 3. August
2018	[Palazzo del Cinema]. In: Werk, Bauen + Wohnen, Nr. 5, S. 36
2019	[Palazzo del Cinema]. In: AS Schweizer Architecture, Nr. 214, S. 25–28
	«L'eredità dell'Accademia in Ticino», in: Archi, Nr. 2, S. 30, 52–53
	[Haus am Elliott Square]. In: Don't Move Improve 2018. New London Architecture. S. 19, 45
	[Leaning Yucca House]. In: Enki, März, S. 63
2020	[Concrete Villa]. In: Raum & Wohnen, Nr. 5, S. 40–50
	[Leaning Yucca House]. In: Focus Archi, Nr. 26, Belgien, S. 65
	[Concrete Villa], «Architects Directory 2020», in: Wallpaper*, Ausgabe Sommer 2020, S. 132

ANDREW CLANCY (TEXTBEITRAG)

Andrew Clancy ist Architekt und Lehrender. Er ist Partner bei Clancy Moore in Dublin, einem Büro, dessen Architektursprache sich aus einer geschickten Auseinandersetzung mit den Rahmenbedingungen und dem Kontext generiert. Die Arbeit des Büros wurde mit zahlreichen nationalen und internationalen Preisen ausgezeichnet und umfassend ausgestellt und publiziert. Seit 2016 ist er Professor für Architektur an der Kingston School of Art (London).

AWARDS

2008	*City of Olten Award* (Diploma project, Mendrisio)
2009	*City of Padova Award* (Diploma project, Mendrisio)
2019	Honourable mention (Concrete Villa, Comano), National Academy of Architecture, Mexico

EXHIBITIONS

2013	*Barcelona_Import Ticino*, COAC Barcelona
2017	*Schweizweit, Recent Architecture in Switzerland*, Swiss Architecture Museum, Basel
	Schweizweit, Recent Architecture in Switzerland, Arc en Rêve, Bordeaux
	Schweizweit, Recent Architecture in Switzerland, Ex-Macello, Lugano
2019	Jalisco Architecture Biennale, Guadalajara
	Transcriptions, From Literary to Architectural Space, Juan Jose Arreola Library, Guadalajara

BIBLIOGRAPHY

2012	Ticino Electrical Company, competition entry, in *Archi*, issue 06/2011, p. 75
2013	Palazzo del Cinema in *Hochparterre*, 01 2013, p. 66
	SAMSTA Chiasso, in *Architects Journal*, May 2013
	Palazzo del Cinema, in *Neue Zürcher Zeitung*, 17.08.2013
	Black House Cagiallo, *Barcelona_Import Ticino, Architecture & Territory*, COAC, p. 72–75
2017	Apartment building in Ascona, in *Schweizweit, Recent Architecture in Switzerland*, Swiss Architecture Museum, p. 86–87
	"Ein architektonisches Meisterwerk sorgt für Glamour am Lago Maggiore", in *Neue Zürcher Zeitung*, 03.08.2017
2018	Palazzo del Cinema, in *Werk, Bauen + Wohnen*, issue 5, Ticino, p. 36
2019	Palazzo del Cinema, in *AS Schweizer Architektur*, issue 214, p. 25–28
	"L'eredità dell'Accademia in Ticino", in *Archi* 2/2019, p. 30, 52–53
	Elliott Square house, in *Don't Move Improve 2018*, New London Architecture, p. 19, 45
	Leaning Yucca house, in *Enki* issue March 2019, p. 63
2020	Concrete Villa, in *Raum & Wohnen*, issue 05/2020, p. 40–50
	Leaning Yucca House, in *Focus Archi*, issue 26, Belgium, p. 65
	Concrete Villa, "Architects Directory 2020", in *Wallpaper**, issue Summer 2020, p. 132

ANDREW CLANCY (ARTICLE)

Andrew Clancy is an architect and educator. He is a partner at Clancy Moore in Dublin, a practice concerned with generating architectural language from a subtle engagement with constraint and context. The office's work has won many national and international awards, and has been extensively exhibited and published. Since 2016, he has been Professor of Architecture at the Kingston School of Art (London).

Finanzielle und ideelle Unterstützung

Ein besonderer Dank gilt den Institutionen und Sponsorfirmen, deren finanzielle Unterstützungen wesentlich zum Erscheinen dieser Buchreihe beitragen. Ihr kulturelles Engagement ermöglicht ein fruchtbares und freundschaftliches Zusammenwirken von Baukultur und Bauwirtschaft.

Financial and conceptual support

Special thanks to the institutions and sponsoring companies whose financial support makes a key contribution to the production of this book series. Their cultural engagement encourages fruitful, friendly interaction between building culture and the building industry.

Schweizerische Eidgenossenschaft
Confédération suisse
Confederazione Svizzera
Confederaziun svizra

Eidgenössisches Departement des Innern EDI
Bundesamt für Kultur BAK

ERNST GÖHNER STIFTUNG

NF ADVISORY, Ascona

Walo Bertschinger SA Ticino, Iragna

A.B. System srl,
Succursale di Chiasso

Alba Building Services Ltd

Alba Building Services Ltd,
London

V-ZUG SA, Bellinzona

ITLAS
IL LEGNO. LA TUA CASA.

ITLAS Srl, Cordignano

JELMONI
INGEGNERIA SA

Jelmoni Ingegneria SA

GMS Building Services Limited,
London

Erisel SA, Bellinzona

WMM Ingenieure AG,
Münchenstein

Resinswiss SA,
Mezzovico

HAMILTON DARCEY LLP

Hamilton Darcey Llp,
London

Estella e Federico Franchini
Carlo De Berti
Forbes Massie, London
Ver3d, Guadalajara
3F Capital

DF_DC
45. Band der Reihe Anthologie
Herausgeber: Heinz Wirz, Luzern
Konzept: Heinz Wirz; DF_DC, Lugano/London
Projektleitung: Quart Verlag, Linus Wirz
Übersetzung Englisch–Deutsch: Miriam Seifert-Waibel, Hamburg
Textlektorat Deutsch: Dr. Eva Dewes, Saarbrücken
Textlektorat Englisch: Benjamin Liebelt, Berlin
Fotos: Simone Bossi, Paris/Mailand S. 11–15, 17–19, 21–23, 45 (6);
Rory Gardiner, London S. 6, 27–29, 44 (3);
Giorgio Marafioti, Paris/Lugano S. 7, 31, 35–37, 43;
DF_DC S. 44 (4, 5)
Visualisierungen: Francesca Petryszak, Bath S. 25, 39–41, 45 (9);
Forbes Massie, London S. 33; DF_DC S. 44 (1, 2);
Ver3d, Guadalajara S. 45 (7, 8, 10)
Redesign: BKVK, Basel – Beat Keusch, Angelina Köpplin-Stützle
Grafische Umsetzung: Quart Verlag
Lithos: Printeria, Luzern
Druck: DZA Druckerei zu Altenburg GmbH, Altenburg

DF_DC
Volume 45 of the series Anthologie
Edited by: Heinz Wirz, Lucerne
Concept: Heinz Wirz; DF_DC, Lugano/London
Project management: Quart Verlag, Linus Wirz
English–German translation: Miriam Seifert-Waibel,
Hamburg
German text editing: Dr. Eva Dewes, Saarbrücken
English text editing: Benjamin Liebelt, Berlin
Photos: Simone Bossi, Paris/Milan p. 11–15, 17–19, 21–23,
45 (6); Rory Gardiner, London p. 6, 27–29, 44 (3);
Giorgio Marafioti, Paris/Lugano p. 7, 31, 35–37, 43;
DF_DC p. 44 (4, 5)
Graphics: Francesca Petryszak, Bath p. 25, 39–41, 45 (9);
Forbes Massie, London p. 33; DF_DC p. 44 (1, 2);
Ver3d, Guadalajara p. 45 (7, 8, 10)
Redesign: BKVK, Basel – Beat Keusch,
Angelina Köpplin-Stützle
Graphical layout: Quart Verlag
Lithos: Printeria, Lucerne
Printing: DZA Druckerei zu Altenburg GmbH, Altenburg

Quart Verlag GmbH
Denkmalstrasse 2, CH-6006 Luzern
books@quart.ch, www.quart.ch

books@quart.ch, www.quart.ch